Be

Fishing

Written by Steve Gilbert
Illustrated by Mike Lacy

HENDERSON
PUBLISHING LTD

© 1992 HENDERSON PUBLISHING LTD

Introduction

Angling is increasingly popular in many countries worldwide. In the United Kingdom, for example, it is the biggest participant sport!

Angling is available to people of all ages and all backgrounds. It can be enjoyed wherever there is stocked waters and in most parts of the world there are waters stocked with various fish that the beginner can catch with little or no trouble.

There are always plenty of older and more experienced anglers who are keen to help and assist the younger and less experienced angler. And within this one sport there are many different methods of fishing that can be tried, dependent on the type of fish stocked and the nature of the venue.

One most important factor to remember is Conservation. The environment and the fish caught must be handled carefully for all to continue to enjoy it. Litter must never be left, particularly tins, glass containers, discarded line and old tackle as this can entrap all kinds of wildlife and even damage other people using the area.

It is important to conserve the fish population so fish may continue to grow and multiply for the further enjoyment of many others. The only exception to this is catching game fish such as trout and salmon which are both caught specifically to be eaten. These are dispatched humanely as soon as they're caught.

The main thing is to enjoy yourselves, being at one with nature in the outdoor environment, pitting your wits against your chosen quarry.

Have fun - tight lines!

Where to fish?

Wherever you choose to fish you must first discover who owns or controls the water. It may be necessary to get permission or a ticket to fish the water. There are many free waters around and these are always very popular with beginners.

The best way to learn is to join an organised angling club with a recognised and thriving junior section. This will give the beginner the benefit of knowledge and experience of much more experienced anglers who are dedicated to encouraging junior anglers.

River Fishing

There are a wide variety of rivers available, some flow very fast and others hardly flow at all. They hold different species of fish depending on the nature and flow of the river.

Faster flowing rivers in most cases contain game fish. The best rivers for the beginner are the slower rivers, or those which are much wider with almost no flow at all.

Take great care when close to any water, particularly flowing rivers, as there is always a danger of falling in and getting into serious trouble.

STILL WATER FISHING

1) Reservoirs :
Man-made lakes for the storage of water for human consumption usually in a chosen valley with an existing natural valley lake. A dam is constructed and the whole valley flooded either naturally or by pumped water transfer from other sources.

Because they are usually very large they will be shared with other water-using groups, eg. boating, windsurfing, water-skiing, etc. They can be very deep and have dangerously steep sides. Areas allocated for angling are usually the safer, shallow beach type areas.

2) Gravel Pits : After the extraction of gravels not all the sites are returned to nature, but some are stocked and turned over to angling. Again as a commercial venture the venue may be shared with similar water-users as with the reservoirs. Depth can vary quite a lot from several metres to less than a metre. A much wider variety of species prosper in this type of venue.

3) Ponds : These exist everywhere - in the country and can either be a man-made feature or a natural occurrence. Many farms have ponds and there is another advantage in that they can also be a valuable source of bait. These are generally very safe and very popular where they are made available to youngsters.

4) Purpose-built Venues : Several types are available and in this a canal, made for boat passage, can be considered as a long, winding and narrow still water. There are also several purpose-built waters that are stocked and double up as a fishing venue. The rowing lane ropes are either removed or dropped to the bottom and hey-presto! you have an instant fishing lake.

TACKLE

Float Rod : There is a great variety of these now available in the shops. Prices vary a great deal but the top of the range rods are for the serious match angler. The beginner will have just as much success and fun with a cheaper float rod. They are normally in three sections with the rings through which the line is threaded spaced in such a way as to maximise the power of the rod. The handle is usually made of cork and will have a reel fitted on it.

Leger Rod : Normally shorter and in two sections. The handle with reel grip is very similar to the float rod.

The last 9"-12" of the rod can be very sensitive to indicate bites. This type of rod is a quiver tip rod, a rod with its own in-built bite indication. The top rings on other leger rods have a screwed connection to take a variety of bite indication equipment. A screw-in quiver tip or swing tip can be used, this gives a variety of uses from the same rod.

Pole : There is a wide variety of poles to choose from these days. The length of the poles can vary from small 1′ metre whips to poles in excess of 14′ metres. The price of these poles can also vary from a few pounds to several thousand pounds. With current material technology the beginner needs to spend very little to enjoy this very enjoyable area of angling. It is a very simple and productive way to fish, especially with younger anglers and beginners.

There are no reels or rings with poles, the line being directly attached to the end of the pole.

The shorter poles, up to 7 metres in length, are called "whips" and the line is attached directly to the end, the fishing being played by the light whip action of the pole. The longer poles have an internal elastic system which can play larger fish using the stretch of elastic of various strengths.

Specimen Rods : Usually of a much stronger composition, all the rods being tested to a particular "test curve". This test curve value will dictate the use to which the rod is put. It may be for any specimen fish.

Reels

There are several kinds of reels available, most commonly used are fixed spool reels. The price range is considerable. Bottom of the range models are quite adequate for the young beginner.

Casting is simple with this type of reel which is important for the beginner. Spare spools can be purchased for the same reel so a variety of fishing methods can be used with the same reel. One spool can be loaded with 2lb breaking strain line for fishing, 3lb line for legering or 10lb line for predator fishing

Centre pin reels are used for fly fishing and on some occasions for stick float fishing in running water.

A variation on the fixed spool reel is the closed-face reel for use in float fishing on either still or running water.

Line

Monofilament line is commonly available in many breaking strains from 3/4lb - 20lb for coarse fishing. For the young beginner 2lb line for float fishing and 3lb for legering.
It is very good as it is very fine in relation to its breaking strain so the fish cannot see it.

Floats

Many types of floats are available and all have their uses at different times in different places. The most common ones are:- Waggler, Stick float, Pole float and Bubble float .

Wagglers

Wagglers are attached bottom end only by locking shots either side of the eye. They are useful on still waters and slow moving waters, able to catch fish at all depths and on the drop.

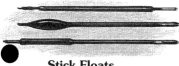

Stick Floats

Used on running water with line attached by float rubbers top and bottom. It is attached in this way so that it can be controlled carefully through fast water.

Pole Floats

These are quite small compared to the previous two floats and have fine bristles to detect bites. They are extremely sensitive and are used in conjunction with poles.

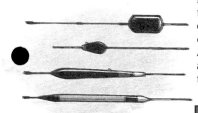

Bubble Floats

Very popular for presenting floating baits for fish such as carp and bleak. Easy to use and a fun way of fishing.

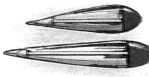

Leger Weights and Shot

Now all made of lead free materials, available from all shops. Both will be needed in a variety of sizes.

Hooks

Always buy and use barbless or micro-barb hooks, sizes 6-22 will be needed depending on the type of fishing that is being undertaken.

Other things that will be needed are bank stakes, keep net, landing net, tackle box, seat box, disgorger, bait tins, catapult and umbrella. All these things are available at your local tackle shop.

SPECIES OF FISH

Barbel

These fish like fast flowing rivers and are very powerful fighters. They are very streamlined which help them to maintain their position against the current. They vary in colour from bronze to green.

A very distinctive feature are the four barbules that hang down around the mouth. They are to be found in clean water flowing over gravel. They also like streamer weed, this gives them good cover and can provide them with food.

Bleak

These are very plentiful on many waters and the fact that they are easy to catch makes them very popular with beginners. They are usually found in very large shoals and offer good sport. They usually feed on the surface or very close to it. They are always found in running water.

Bream

a) Common Bream

These are the favourite quarry of many pleasure anglers and match anglers. They prefer still waters or very slow moving waters but also feature on some fast flowing rivers in the quieter, slacker areas.

They are a shoal fish and when catching them it is quite common to observe that they are all the same size as they are most likely the result of one spawning.

They have a deep, flat body that earns them the nickname of "slab" and a hump that earns them the nickname "Humphrey". Young bream, better known as "skimmers", are silver in colour but adult fish can vary in colour from bronze to almost black in some venues.

They are bottom feeders and a spell of close observation can reveal muddy water or streams of bubbles from the bottom where they are feeding. A ravenous shoal of bream would need quite a lot of bait to be introduced to hold them in one area.

b) Silver Bream

These are extremely rare and to catch one is quite an event. Many people mistake "skimmer" common bream wrongly for silver bream. They are usually only caught in smaller waters such as farm ponds.

Roach

Probably the most common of all fish and very popular with anglers as they are usually present in very large numbers in a variety of waters. They are a shoal fish and many can be caught in one session with practice. Their nickname is "Red-Fin" due to their distinctive red fins which contrast with the silver body of the fish. This is probably one of the fish that the young angler will pursue. They can also hybridise with common bream and this hybrid are hard fighting, formidable fish to catch.

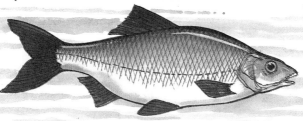

Perch

Very similar to the roach in as much that they are common in a whole variety of venues. They are distinguished by dark vertical strips down the body which is green at the top becoming lighter further down the body of the fish. They have sharp dorsal fins. The nickname of this fish is "stripey". They are also shoal fish with the chance of catching many of them in one session.

Tench

The tench prefers the same habitats as the common bream, still or slow moving waters. They are very powerful fighting fish and are very popular with both pleasure and match anglers. Their colour is a dark olive green with distinctive red eyes. They are usually caught more in the warmer summer months but can sometimes provide a surprise to the angler in the depths of winter.

They are a very powerful fish with tiny scales and a thick coating of mucous (slime). This makes them very smooth to the feel.
All the fins are well rounded.

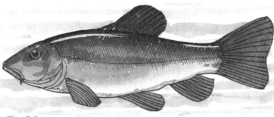

Rudd

These are very similar to roach and are a very popular summer fish. They are a golden colour with the larger fish looking like slabs of gold. They like to surface feed so they have a protruding bottom lip to enable them to feed off insects and other food from the surface.

Young roach and rudd may be difficult to tell apart but the rudd has its golden colour from an early age.

Carp

There are four types of carp commonly caught by the angler. They are quite similar to bream in that they prefer slow moving and still waters. They grow well in very weedy environments with muddy bottoms.

Common carp are fully scaled, usually of a very golden colour. They can vary in shape from the long streamlined torpedo shape of smaller fish to a much deeper body when they have matured.

Leather carp has no scales whatsoever and is the rarest of the carp family.

Mirror carp tend to be more orange but have only a few quite large scales on their body. They tend to have a row along the body.

Crucian carp are a more popular fish with young anglers as they do not reach the larger size of the rest of the carp family, 2kg vs. 20kg! It is a much shorter fish and is deep-bodied. They tend to be shoal fish and respond well to more conventional angling rather than the specimen tactics that have to be used to catch its larger relatives.

Chub

These fish are great lovers of flowing water as a natural habitat but can adapt to a still water environment if introduced by man. They are golden green in colour, fully scaled. They have extremely large mouths and virtually take any bait. Caution must be taken when unhooking them as they have a sharp set of teeth in their throat. They feed throughout the year in most of the environments.

Pike

This is a powerful predatory fish which is equipped with sharp, needle-like teeth. The colouring of greens and yellow is good to enable them to camouflage themselves. They eat almost any fish that they can get in their mouth and have also been known to take small water birds. Great care must be used when unhooking them as the teeth are capable of inflicting nasty wounds on any angler.

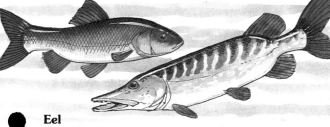

Eel

The eel quite resembles a snake and looks like no other fish. They are dark green in colour and feed on the bottom of almost any habitat. They are very difficult to unhook and can also tangle the tackle of an angler either young or old.

BAITS

Fish themselves feed on a wide variety of things depending on their habitat and type. It is very important that the bait most likely to catch your chosen fish is used at the right time. The most popular baits that are used are as follows:-

Maggots

These are widely available from many outlets and are bred commercially in a large way. A maggot is the larval stage of various flies. They are available in a variety of shapes, sizes and colours.

extremely soft, white maggot that is a very popular bait for bream fishing. Because of the work involved in breeding this specific maggot only the dedicated match fisherman will bother to breed them.

b) Maggots :
The normal hook maggots are the larval stage of the bluebottle. They are available in a wide variety of colours. They can be red, blue, bronze, yellow, fluorescent and any other colour depending on the maggot breeder's imagination.

Each type of maggot has a specific role in angling as follows:-

a) Gozzers :

These are usually bred at home and not usually available from tackle shops. They are an

c) Pinkies :

These are much smaller maggots and are the larval stage of the greenbottle. Mainly used as feed either introduced by catapult, hand or in groundbait. Can also be used on the hook singly or in pairs to catch fish on days when they will not take maggots.

These are also available in a variety of colours.

d) Squats :

These are much smaller than pinkies and are used commonly in groundbait for bream fishing. They are also available in a variety of colours.

The advantage of using squat instead of pinkies is that unlike pinkies they do not try to bury in the mud but remain on top or the bottom for fish to feed on. They can be used on the smaller hook sizes, when the fishing is hard, as a tempting hook bait.

e) Casters :

When maggots turn from the larval stage to the chrysalis stage they are called casters. This has been a very important bait over the years. It is an extremely important additive to groundbait to hold feeding fish and a very successful hookbait, particularly when fishing for roach.

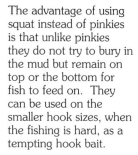

Normal casters from the tackle shop are those that sink through the water and stay on the bottom. It is very often useful in the summer to have some floating casters to catch surface feeding roach, rudd, etc.

Natural baits, which all can work in various situations, include the following:-

a) Slugs : A very popular bait when presented on a large hook for chub and eels.

b) Elderberries : These will account for roach and chub in habitats where elder bushes overhang the river.

c) Lobworms : Can be pulled from home lawn, a good bait for virtually all coarse fish if presented on a large hook.

Redworms
Very common bait used by many anglers. Easily bred at home in the compost heap, turning it into a wormery. A very popular bait for most types of coarse fish.

Brandlings
Known by some as "tiger-worms" due to yellow bands around their body. Can be bred in a wormery as the redworm but types can be bought from tackle shops.

Bread baits

Bread can be fished in many ways and will catch almost all types of coarse fish except the predators:-

a) Bread Paste : This is made using bread minus the crust. It is soaked then worked into a paste that can be used on the hook.

c) Bread Crust :
This is used differently to flake and paste. The crust is usually taken with a little white bread attached and fished as a floating bait.
It can either be surface fished or as a buoyant bait off the bottom anchored by a leger weight.

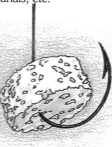

b) Bread Flake :
Again the white part of the bread is used. A piece is pinched from the slice or loaf which is nipped onto the shank of a fairly large hook, the rest is left fluffy with the point of the hook visible.

d) Bread Punch :
Pellets of bread are punched from a slice of bread and removed from the bread punch onto a hook. Usually associated with catching small fish in hard fished areas such as canals, etc.

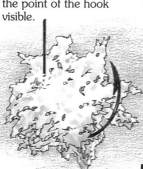

Meat baits

A variety of meats are used to catch a wide range of fish. Luncheon meat is the most popular with most anglers. The hook is pushed through a cube of meat and the hook turned to prevent it pulling back or anchored with a piece of grass between the bend and the meat.

Sweetcorn

Now a very popular bait for roach, bream, chub, carp and tench particularly. Very easy to obtain from any shop either tinned or frozen.

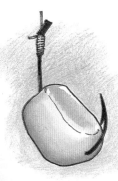

Cheese

Any cheese can be rolled into a paste and if fished on a large hook will tempt chub particularly.

Seed baits

Hemp, tare, wheat and barley once cooked and tender are extremely good baits and they can account for fish, usually better fish when most other baits don't work.

Groundbait

This is available in dry form from all tackle shops. There is a wide variety available with uses for different waters, fish and conditions. It is mixed with water until it can be rolled into a ball that stays together if thrown until it hits the water.

A variety of other feed can be mixed in. Pinkies, squatts, casters, sweetcorn, hemp, chopped worms can all be added depending on the fish, water and conditions. The white and brown groundbait is made from finely crushed or ground breadcrumbs.

The new range of groundbaits and additives all have different flavours and consistencies for a variety of venues and fish. If too much is used it can overfeed the fish and they will not take the anglers hookbait. If too little groundbait is used then a shoal of hungry fish move off in search of food in a different area.

FLOAT FISHING

There are many kinds of float fishing depending on whether a still or running water is being fished, or whether the water is deep or shallow. When using a float, fish can be caught at any depth from the surface to the bottom.

Some floats are fished "top and bottom"; these are quills, avons or stick floats and they are fished mainly on running waters. Other floats are fished bottom end only, being fixed in position by shots locked either side of their bottom eye. They are called darts, wagglers and zoomers.

Floats are made from a variety of materials. Quills can be made from any large bird feathers. Many modern floats, particularly the modern stepped wagglers, are made from transparent plastic. Anglers often have at least two of each particular float so that if one is lost or broken whilst using it successfully they can immediately set up the identical float.

Wagglers

These are extremely versatile floats that can be used on both still and slower running water. The varieties of waggler available are bodied wagglers and straight wagglers. Both can be bought in "stepped" set up for sensitivity reasons. These are probably used more than any other float.

The larger varieties that carry most weight can be cast great distances and yet still offer sensitive registration of bites. The most modern loaded waggler have a large proportion of the weight needed to cock them incorporated in the float so that only a few weights are needed to set them up and this weight is normally printed on the float. When fishing the bottom with a waggler it is important to set up the depth accurately.

The float is locked both sides of the eye then the bulk of the shot about halfway to the hook then a small shot (size 8 or 10) about 18" from the hook. This shot is known as the "trigger shot" or "tell-tale". When the correct amount of shot has been added, cock the float with only a small amount of tip showing. A plummet is attached to the hook and the float cast into the chosen area.

If the float goes under then the float must be moved up by moving the shots. This means that the plummet is on the bottom. If the float is sitting higher than before it was plumbing the depth and the "tell-tale" shot is on the bottom.

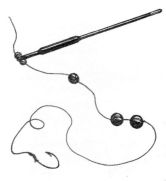

Ideally the hook and bait should be on the bottom with the "tell-tale" shot clear of the bottom.

Once the float is set up scatter some loose offerings around the float to attract fish into the area you are going to fish. If the chosen line is near then the "loose feed" can be thrown in and if fished at longer range a catapult is used. Take care to cast the float in the same position each time and the "loose feed" in exactly the same place.

To cast, the float is reeled to within 2 feet of the top of the rod and the bale arm of the reel undone and the line held on the spool with a finger. The rod is swept over the head in a sweeping movement, releasing the finger holding the line on the spool when the rod is at the top.

Just before the float hits the water the line is trapped again with the finger. This ensures that the line below the float hits the water neatly behind the float. The tip of the rod is put under the water and the reel turned until all the line from rod tip to float is buried under the water. This makes sure that the float doesn't drift about in the wind.

When a fish takes the bait the float will normally go under or slide away slowly. If a fish picks the bait up and lifts the "tell-tale" shot then the float lifts up. This is called a "lift bite".

You must strike into the fish and start to gently reel it towards you. If it is small it can be swung in and if large, it can be guided into a landing net.

If you are not getting bites a change of bait may be needed. Maggots are usually hooked lightly in the blunt end. Casters are best fished with the hook buried in it. Sweetcorn can be hooked in several ways as can all the types of worm. Never be afraid to make a bait change. Watch those around you who are catching fish and if you aren't catching any, take note of what range they are fishing at, where the shots are, how big the hook is, what bait is being used and what pattern of feeding is in use. Then go back to your own place and imitate the way that they are fishing. You should start catching fish as well.

Remove the hook from the fish's mouth with fingers or by disgorger if fish are awkwardly hooked.

Stick float

These are used in fast running water and attached top and bottom with "float rubbers". The shotting varies according to the flow and depth. When used on gentler flows the weight should be evenly spaced down the line.

The float should usually be adjusted to the right depth by moving it up or down by moving the line through the float rubbers. It should be set so that it just trips along the bottom.

Feed should be introduced on the line that the float is going down the water. The float will go down the fed line and will be some distance along before bites are seen.

The fish will probably be caught at the same point through the swim each time. The float is usually fished quite close to the bank, that is 1 to 2 rod lengths, and this enables it to be controlled by controlling the speed that the line is allowed to come off the reel. Maggots and casters are most commonly used as hook bait for this method that will give good bags of chub, roach and dace.

When a fish takes the bait the float may not always go under but may do something different. To strike into the fish the finger that has been controlling the line from the spool must be applied to the spool then a clean strike of the rod to contact the fish. The bale arm is then closed by turning the handle a little - the fish can then be played back along the current to the landing net.

Avons

These are another running water float usually taking much more weight than floats with large balsa bodies.

They can be used in slightly faster water. They can also carry much larger baits than stick floats.

Bubble floats

These are quite popular for catching surface feeding fish in the summer. The line through to the hook is passed through either one or two eyes in the bubble float and can be locked off with two small shots. The depth that the float is in the water can be varied by slightly filling the float with water. They have small removable bungs that allow the angler to do this. A variety of fish using a variety of baits and hook sizes can be caught by this method.

The float does not usually indicate a bite but watching the actual bait or the line between the float and the bait does. Bleak, dace and rudd can be taken using a bubble float with a size 16-22 hook with maggot or floating caster.

If the hook is changed for a 6-12 the bait can be bread flake, bread crust or dog mixer biscuit then the quarry will be carp or chub. This is a very interesting method for the beginner with patience.

If loose offerings are thrown in to attract large carp and the offering on the hook cast amongst them, often the fish will take all the loose offerings and ignore the one with the hook in.

This may happen many times but eventually a fish will become over-confident and take the offering with the hook in. If you have the patience for this then you should manage the other methods successfully in due course.

Leger fishing

This is generally the method used to fish a static bait. There are different sorts of indicators on a rod to record the bites and various terminal tackle set ups that are all equally effective if used in the right conditions.

Various weights can be used to anchor the bait on the river bed or a swim feeder or maggot feeder can be used. This has the advantage of feeding the swim at the same time. There are two basic terminal tackle set ups:-

1) Fixed link Paternoster :

The weight can either be a leger bomb or maggot-groundbait feeder. The length from the link to the weight can be from 6" to 18". The length from the link to the hook can vary from 1' to 9' depending on the water and conditions. The groundbait and maggot feeders can carry the same weight as the bomb, this varies from 1/8oz to 2oz (3-50 grams).

The choice of weight is totally dependent on the flows involved and the distance to be cast.

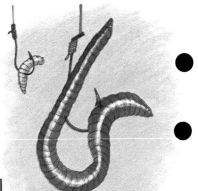

This set up is the most popular with pleasure and match anglers. The size of hook used can vary from a size 2 to a size 26! The larger hook baited with bread baits, lobworms, slugs, etc. will catch large carp, bream, perch and chub.

The smaller hooks baited with maggot, pinkie, squat or bloodworm will take bags of smaller juvenile fish of various species. If a snap link is fitted to the leger bomb link then a quick change can be made from leger weight to maggot feeder or groundbait feeder.

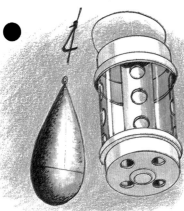

The length of line from the leger link to the hook is called the "tail". If you are missing bites with the bait being damaged, then increase the tail length. This will normally result in fish being cleanly hooked.
If fish are deep hooked then the tail length is shortened so the bites are seen much sooner.

2) Running Leger :

This is a simple rig with the line going through the bomb link or feed link and the hook being attached to the end. A shot, usually a No.1 or No.4, stops the leger weight sliding down to the hook.
Reposition the shot to change the tail length. Different sorts of weight are used this way, either coffin leads or drilled bullets in a variety of weights can be used.

Groundbait is mixed up for open end feeders and laced with a variety of baits such as maggots, casters, pinkies, squatts and hemp. Block end feeders are used in faster flowing waters so they have the chance of getting to the bottom before they unload.

While legering ...
This is a part of the rod or a rod attachment. Types available are:-

1) Quiver Tip Rods In several lengths from "wands" as short as 6'-7' up to 'feeder rods' that can be 10'-11' in length. The most popular is 9'-10'. They normally have a through action but the bite is indicated by the top 15"-18". Its sensitivity depends upon the flow. A still water quiver tip is very sensitive whereas one for use in a strong current has to be much stiffer. After casting to a consistent spot, the quiver tip falls back when the weight hits the bottom. The line is then tightened to the bomb from the tip of the rod by turning the reel handle. A slight curve is left in the tip so that if the fish moves with the baited hook away from the rod, the tip will move round and the angler must strike into the fish and play it in in the usual manner.
With tension on the tip, if a fish takes the baited hook and moves toward the rod then the tip will fall back. Again the angler must strike. This is called a "drop-back" bite.

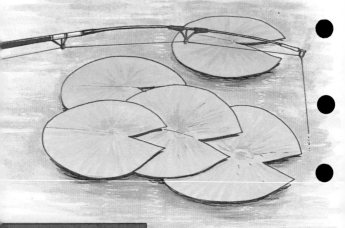

2) Swing Tip Rods : A swing tip rod will usually double up as a quiver tip rod. This is because the top ring has a threaded end to accept a screw-in swing tip or screw-in quiver tip. Leger rods are about 9'-10' long. The swing tip can vary in length from 9" to 18" and the screw-in piece is connected to the swing tip with a piece of rubber. When it is screwed into the leger rod it swings free, hence its name.

Cast with the leger weight as usual and while the weight is falling the swing tip points out straight to the water. When the weight hits the bottom the swing tip falls back. The line is gradually tightened to the weight with the reel until the tip is at 45 degrees. It will record bites when the fish takes the bait and moves away by lifting up and if the fish picks up the bait and moves toward the angler then it drops back - another "drop-back" bite. This is not useful in fast running water as the tip will be pulled out too tight and detection of bites will be almost impossible. It is very sensitive and the fish feel the resistance of a swing tip much less than a quiver tip.

3) Butt Indicator : It attaches between the bottom ring and next to bottom ring of a leger rod. A normal cast is made but the tip is buried in the water pointing towards the baited area. The line is tightened to the weight in the normal way until the indicator is at its halfway point. Now both types of bite will be registered.

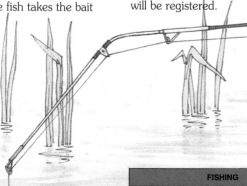

POLE FISHING

The shortest poles can be as short as 1´ metre and the longest in excess of 19 metres! The cost variation is a few pounds to several thousand pounds for the other end of the range. They can be used to catch small fish at great speed or contact, play and land many other fish into double figures.

There are two quite distinct methods of pole fishing, firstly short pole or "whip" that is up to 7 metres in length and then the long pole technique, that is a pole longer than 7 metres.

1) Short Pole or "Whip" Fishing

There are no reels or rings and it is a simple and quick method that all can enjoy.

Most "whips" are telescopic so they can be extended to their full length in seconds. There are various numbers of sections depending on the type and cost of the "whip".

The beginner can start at the very bottom end of the cost range and enjoy good sport for very little cost. Any "whip" from 3 to 7 metres is suitable in length for a beginner.

The end sections of whips are very fine and bend so as to play any fish that may be caught. Some have the top section or top two sections modified to take an elastic system.

This would be best described as short pole fishing when using elastic as this does a similar job to using a very "whippy" end section. The elastic system will be described in greater depth in the long pole section. The making of pole rigs, their storage, selection and use will appear later after the section on pole fishing.

2) Long Pole Fishing

These poles are taken apart and depending on the type they are either "put in" or "put over" joints depending on whether the joints go over or in each other. They must usually be broken down, that is the joints taken apart to land a fish once hooked whereas the short pole or "whip" technique is fished to hand as the length of line is chosen so that when a fish is swung in it comes to hand.

A long pole can be held in two hands slightly apart and the pole weight rested on one knee whilst seated on a box. Another way is to use a set of pole rests to support the pole so that two hands are available to put in feed either by hand or by catapult. This is in direct contrast to whip fishing which is predominantly one-handed leaving the other hand free to loose feed from a bait supply that is normally kept in an apron worn by the angler, a must for this type of fishing.

3) Pole Rigs

These vary according to the type of venue being fished, type of fish to be caught and the length of pole to be used. These rigs are usually made up at home as it would be very difficult to shot and set up accurately such sensitive floats on the bankside. A piece of line is attached to the float in a tall container of water and various shots added to the line until the float is sensitively set with a minimum of tip showing.

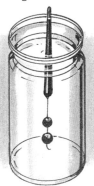

The bulk of the weight is added in the form of an olivette. This is a torpedo shaped weight with a hole through the middle through which the line passes.

The position of the olivette in relation to the hook is set by a weight upon which it sits. If it is necessary to make the bait fall slowly through the water then the olivette is set close under the float.

If the fish are feeding hard on the bottom, an olivette is set closer to the hook length so the baited hook is taken down to the feeding fish as soon as possible. The length of line used from the pole and the hook equals the depth of water plus a short length of line from the float to the end of the pole. Rigs are wound onto winders and stored in winder boxes.

Keep a number of rigs with different sized floats, hooks and hook lengths made up so that you have a wide choice available. Many match anglers have several hundred rigs!

Further essentials

Elastic strength used varies according to the angler's quarry. If small fish are to be caught and the long pole with elastic is preferred to the straight "whip" then a very light elastic is used. If the quarry is the larger species of fish then a very heavy elastic will be used. Tackle shops will set up the 'elastication' in end sections on request but it is quite easy to do if all the necessary parts are purchased.

Whip fishing for small or large surface feeding fish is an art on its own. A small float which requires around 1 x No.8 shot only should be used. The float carries its 1 x No.8 shot under it and then there is no shot between the float and hook, usually a distance of half a metre. Some loose offerings are thrown in, then the float is cast overhead into the feeding area.

This method will take fish off the top, either very small roach, rudd, etc or sort out quality roach, rudd and perch. This can be a very good method particularly in early to late evening.

On most waters it is essential to plumb the depth and set the pole rig just on the bottom. If with steady feeding this produces no fish the depth can be adjusted so that the bait is laying on the bottom or just clear of the bottom.
If there is no success with this then all the weight except for 1 x No.8 shot half a metre from the hook is put directly under the float.

This has the effect of letting the bait sink very slowly from surface to bottom. This will identify if the fish are feeding somewhere in mid water.

PREDATOR FISHING

All predators such as pike, zander and large perch are all common quarry for this area of angling.

The best time for predator fishing is from early Autumn through to early Spring. A strong rod is required as the fish can run to as much as 40lb. Line should be no less than 10lb, preferably 15lb.

A steel trace is used to ensure that the fish does not bite through the line.

Plugs and Lures

This is the use of an artificial lure and moving it in such a way that the fish is tempted to attack it. Treble hooks are attached to the lure, plug or spinner. Spinners can just be shaped pieces of metal painted in various colours usually to imitate a fish. They may have flowing tails or even be designed to make some sort of noise and spin around as they move through the water.

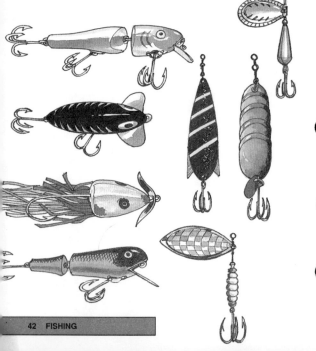

Plugs and lures come in a wide variety of shapes, sometimes made of wood, metal or plastic. They also are fashioned and painted in such a way as to imitate a fish. They are all cast past the suspected feeding area of the fish and retrieved in various ways.

They can be brought back steadily or in a draw and sink fashion to tempt the fish to attack it.

Remember - you should always be accompanied by an experienced angler who is used to catching and handling predators.

PREDATOR FISHING

Dead Bait
Most popular are sea baits such as sprat, mackerel and smelt.

Also popular are some dead coarse fish, particularly small trout. These can be attached to pairs of treble hooks and be legered or float fished.

Using the bait method it is important to strike early enough so that the fish will not be too deeply hooked. These fish make many powerful lunging runs and they must be carefully played.

Essential items are:-
1) Large landing net
2) Unhooking mat
3) Disgorging forceps (artery-type)
4) Gardening type gloves

Large landing nets are important, also an unhooking mat so the fish will not be damaged. Hooks are carefully removed using forceps whilst holding the lower jaw externally with gardening glove.

One big advantage of fishing for both trout and salmon is that you can take them home and eat them at the end of the day. Very tasty they are too!

Trout rods are generally shorter and much more "whippy" than their coarse angling counterparts. A centre pin reel is used and it can be loaded with a variety of lines. There are very many types all with different uses for different situations. This is again an area of angling that a beginner cannot tackle on their own straight away. Lessons are very often available at the more aware trout fisheries.

The choice of fly is the most important aspect of this sport. It is no use offering one particular fly when all over the water another particular type of fly is hatching and trout are feeding voraciously on that. When a fish has been caught and killed ready for subsequent removal to home and cooking, the contents of the stomach are spooned. This involves inserting a spoon into the fish's mouth and removing the contents of the stomach. This will clearly identify what that particular trout had been feeding on and could well influence the choice of fly to be used.

Casting: The line is usually already pulled from the reel and can be on the floor in front of the angler or in a special tray worn at belt height and the line laid in there.

Most people start their game fishing career on large stocked reservoirs. The fish generally introduced into these are called "stockies".

They are generally between 3/4lb and 1lb. They can grow on in these very food rich environments to be caught years later at very good weights. Brown trout and rainbow trout are stocked and one or two waters are now introducing salmon into lakes.

THE BIG CATCH

Most people like to progress to catching predator fish in what is a natural habitat for them, that is fairly shallow, fast running water found in mountainous or hilly regions.

The angler stands in the water and allows a fly to go down with the stream into an area and above where rising fish have been seen. This is a very good side of this sport but great care must be taken. You must always be accompanied by a more experienced angler who knows the area very well.

Underwater rocks can become very slippery when covered with weed and there may be deep holes in rivers that look generally very shallow. In deeper water if an angler goes in and thigh boots fill with water then rescue can become very difficult.

Keep safety in mind, and there can be nothing nicer than to catch fresh trout and salmon from a running water. Taking them home to prepare for the table will give the angler pleasure yet again!